First Facts™

From Farm to Table

From Wheat to Bread

by Kristin Thoennes Keller

Consultant:
Golden Wave Chapter of Kansas
Women Involved in Farm Economics (WIFE)

Capstone
press

Mankato, Minnesot

First Facts is published by Capstone Press
151 Good Counsel Drive, P.O. Box 669, Mankato, Minnesota 56002
www.capstonepress.com

Library of Congress Cataloging-in-Publication Data
Thoennes Keller, Kristin.
    From wheat to bread / by Kristin Thoennes Keller.
    p. cm.—(First facts. From farm to table)
    Includes bibliographical references (p. 23) and index.
    ISBN 0-7368-2638-6 (hardcover)
    1. Bread. [1. Bread.] I. Title. II. Series.
TX769.T453 2005
664'.7523—dc22   2003023375

Summary: An introduction to the basic concepts of food production, distribution, and consumption
    by tracing the production of bread from wheat to the finished product.

Editorial Credits
Roberta Schmidt, editor; Jennifer Bergstrom, designer; Kelly Garvin, photo researcher; Eric Kudalis,
    product planning editor

Photo Credits
Capstone Press/Gary Sundermeyer, front cover, 5, 19
Corbis/Jacqui Hurst, 14; John Hulme: Eye Ubiquitous, 15
David R. Frazier Photolibrary, 16–17
Grant Heilman Photography/Larry Lefever, 10–11, 12–13
Photo by Jim Scott, Wheatweaving Company, 20
PhotoDisc Inc., back cover, 1 (all); C. Borland/PhotoLink 2000, 6–7
Richard Hamilton Smith, 9
Visuals Unlimited/Inga Spence, 8

1 2 3 4 5 6 09 08 07 06 05 04

Table of Contents

Eating Bread

Many people eat bread every day. Bread can be flat or raised. Flat bread is like a soft taco shell. Raised bread is spongy. Many people use slices of raised bread to make sandwiches.

Bread has to be made before people can eat it. Making bread takes many steps.

Fun Fact!
People in Egypt first baked raised bread more than 5,000 years ago.

Grain

Bread can be made from different kinds of **grains**. A grain is a small seed that is eaten or planted. Wheat is one kind of grain. Bread is often made from wheat.

Fun Fact!
Corn, rice, oats, barley, and rye are other types of grains.

Growing Wheat

Young wheat looks like green grass. As wheat grows, **kernels** form at the top of the stems. When the wheat turns yellow, it is ready to be cut.

Farmers use **combines** to cut
the wheat. Combines separate the
kernels from the stems, or straw.
The kernels are put into big trucks.

Moving Wheat

Trucks carry the wheat kernels to a **grain elevator**. There, the farmers sell the wheat to the elevator company. Food companies buy the wheat from the grain elevator company. Some wheat is sold to other countries.

Fun Fact!
Some people call grain elevators prairie skyscrapers.

Making Flour

Wheat becomes flour at a **mill**. Machines at the mill clean the kernels and **grind** them into flour. If the whole kernel is used, the flour is brown. If only the middle part of the kernel is used, the flour is white. **Vitamins** sometimes are added to the flour.

Fun Fact!
More foods are made with wheat than any other grain.

Baking Bread

Bread companies buy flour. Water, yeast, and other **ingredients** are added to the flour. All of the ingredients are mixed together to make bread dough.

The bread dough rises. It is put into pans and placed in an oven. As the dough bakes, it rises more and turns golden brown. It becomes bread.

To the Store

After the bread cools, it is sliced. Machines and workers then wrap the bread in bags. Bread companies sell the bread to stores. Workers put the bread in trucks for the trip to the stores.

Where to Find Bread

Bread is sold almost everywhere. Grocery stores, drugstores, and some gas stations sell bread. Bakeries make and sell many kinds of bread. Some people even bake their own bread.

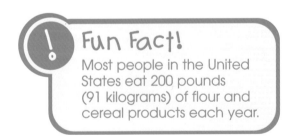

Fun Fact!
Most people in the United States eat 200 pounds (91 kilograms) of flour and cereal products each year.

Wheat can be used to make baskets, dolls, and many other things. Weavers make these items out of the dried wheat stems called straw.

Weavers first soak the straw in water. The water makes the straw easier to bend. Weavers then braid the straw into designs.

Hands On: Colonial Brown Bread

Many kinds of bread are made with yeast. Colonial brown bread is a sweet bread made without yeast. You can make this bread at home. Ask an adult to help you.

What You Need

mixing spoons
measuring cups and spoons
4 cups (960 mL) whole wheat flour
1⅓ cups (320 mL) all-purpose flour
1 cup (240 mL) brown sugar
4 teaspoons (20 mL) baking soda
1 teaspoon (5 mL) salt
large mixing bowl
4 cups (960 mL) buttermilk
2 greased bread pans

What You Do

1. Preheat the oven to 350°F (180°C).
2. Stir the flour, sugar, baking soda, and salt together in a bowl.
3. Add the buttermilk to the bowl. Stir until everything is mixed together.
4. Pour the mixture into the bread pans.
5. Put the pans in the oven. Bake the bread for 1 hour.
6. Serve the bread warm. Keep leftovers in the refrigerator.

Glossary

combine (KOM-bine)—a large farm machine that is used to harvest crops

grain (GRAYN)—the seed of a cereal plant, such as wheat, corn, or rice

grain elevator (GRAYN EL-uh-vay-tur)—a tall, large building used for storing grain

grind (GRINDE)—to crush something into fine pieces

ingredient (in-GREE-dee-uhnt)—an item used to make something else

kernel (KER-nuhl)—the seed of a plant

mill (MIL)—a building that has machines to grind grain into flour

vitamin (VYE-tuh-min)—a nutrient that helps keep people healthy

Read More

Hill, Mary. *Let's Make Bread.* In the Kitchen. New York: Children's Press, 2002.

Jones, Carol. *Bread.* From Farm to You. Philadelphia: Chelsea House, 2003.

Weninger, Brigitte, and Anne Möller. *Good Bread: A Book of Thanks.* New York: North-South Books, 2003.

Internet Sites

FactHound offers a safe, fun way to find Internet sites related to this book. All of the sites on FactHound have been researched by our staff.

Here's how:
1. Visit *www.facthound.com*
2. Type in this special code **0736826386** for age-appropriate sites. Or enter a search word related to this book for a more general search.
3. Click on the **Fetch It** button.

FactHound will fetch the best sites for you!

Index